MW00387539

Summary: Get It Done: A Quantitative Dissertation Template is a book for dissertation students, dissertation committee members, and anyone who wants to understand the entire process in a precise way. If you are looking to quickly understand the quantitative dissertation process, need a template, and/or need a proven plan for you and your dissertation committee members to follow, this book is for you.

This book was based on my personal experiences writing a quantitative dissertation. My understanding of the process started off in much confusion and frustration, With God's help, I was able to understand the entire process and complete my dissertation successfully. My dissertation has received over 800 downloads within three years of being published. This book will show you the lessons that I have learned. Don't waste your precious time trying to figure it all out on your own. Get it done by using this book as your guide.

Link to my published quantitative dissertation:
https://scholarworks.waldenu.edu/cgi/viewcontent.cgi?article=3067&context=dissertations

Get It Done:
A Quantitative
Dissertation Template

Dr. Leslie D'Anjou

Table of Contents

Introduction

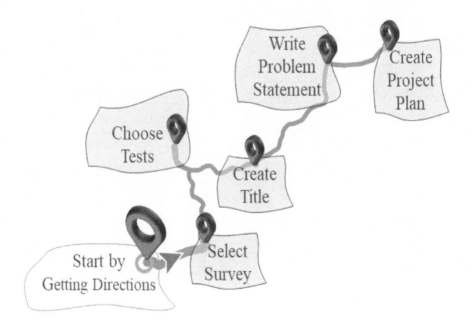

Get It Done: A Quantitative Dissertation Template

Proverbs 3:6 (NIV) In all your ways submit to him, and he will make your paths straight.

Completing a dissertation is never easy. If you submit it to God, He promises he will make your path straight. This quantitative dissertation template is based on a successfully completed dissertation that was submitted to God. I will show you how to have a good starting point, write your chapters with ease, and complete your pages. Don't you dare give up! Using this template will help anyone quickly understand the big picture of completing a quantitative dissertation.

My dissertation process started off in confusion. I searched all kinds of dissertations, books, and articles looking for a complete understanding of the dissertation process with little to no luck. All the resources that my university provided only made it more confusing. As I wrote pieces of my dissertation, my dissertation committee would provide feedback that related to other parts and chapters of the dissertation process that I did not start or know existed. It was frustrating and confusing.

I am sure you can agree that the dissertation process has many moving parts. My University's dissertation process had three major parts. First, I had to get approval for my prospectus (title, problem statement, and part of Chapter 1), Secondly, I had to develop and defend the proposal (Chapter's 1, 2, & 3). Finally, I had to develop and defend the entire dissertation (Chapter's 1 thru 5). These three major parts, in my mind, could easily take years to complete and understand. I could not see it initially as three simple parts. All I could think about is how will I ever complete 100+ pages and graduate. The task was daunting.

I wanted to know the entire process and what I needed to do. I got to the point where I became so frustrated with the process that I decided to write my entire dissertation in one week. I wanted to understand the entire process and get it done. I found a published dissertation from my university that related to a topic I wanted to focus on. I followed that dissertation's layout from start to finish. With much grit and determination, I completed my first unofficial dissertation within a week.

There was a problem with my approach. I bypassed my University's three-major-parts process. My Dissertation Chair and Committee Member were baffled. They asked, when did you get approval for the prospectus or the proposal? When did you get approval from the Internal Review Board (IRB) to conduct this research? I nervously said I did not get approval. I just wanted to understand the entire process and get it done. They told me that I had violated our University's dissertation process and that they would be reporting this violation. I was scared and nervous. A violation could mean that I could possibly get kicked out of our University and waste all my time, effort, and money. I got down on my knees and prayed for help.

My University came back with a decision. They said that my dissertation was an unsanctioned dissertation and I won't be able to use the dataset at all. Fortunately for me, I used secondary data to complete my initial dissertation. They wrote that I can use everything except for the dataset. This was sad but great news. I got the chance to understand the entire dissertation process. All I had to do then was to replace my secondary dataset with an approved primary dataset. Finally, I got a better understanding of the dissertation process. From that point forward, I was able to complete my dissertation within a year.

This dissertation template provides you with a high-level guide to help you complete your dissertation and understand the entire process holistically. You must understand where to start and how to build a solid foundation.

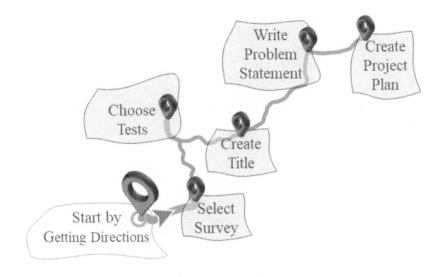

Starting Point:
1. Get Directions: Write down your university's dissertation heading requirements
2. Select a survey or prior experiment
3. Choose your main tests
4. Create a title
5. Write your problem statement
6. Create a project plan

Below is a quick snapshot of my university's quantitative dissertation heading requirements in chronological order.

- Cover Page
- Abstract Page
- Dedication Page
- Acknowledgment Pages
- Table of Contents Page
- List of Tables Page(s)
- List of Figures Page(s)
- Chapter 1: Introduction to the Study
- Chapter 2: Literature Review
- Chapter 3: Research Method
- Chapter 4: Results
- Chapter 5: Discussion, Conclusions, and Recommendations
- References
- Appendix A: Consent Forms
- Appendix B: Survey Questions
- Appendix C: Letter of Recruitment
- Appendix D: Participant Reminder E-mail
- Appendix E: Acknowledgement Consent Form

1. **Get Directions:** Write down your University's Dissertation
   Heading Requirements:

Note: A simple way to find this list is to find a quantitative
dissertation from your university that was published within the past
year. List all the main headings of that dissertation.

- _____
- _____
- _____
- _____
- _____
- _____
- _____
- _____
- _____
- _____
- _____
- _____
- _____
- _____
- _____
- _____
- _____
- _____
- _____

Helpful Writing Tips:
Now that you have listed your university's heading requirements, you can continue the process of completing your dissertation with purpose. I have provided you with some writing tips to help you complete your dissertation with the right frame of mind. Always start from a high-level perspective and then get granular.

When writing, you should always be thinking in terms of the main idea (title/topic), headings, subheadings, paragraphs, and sentences. If you ever find yourself stuck on what to write, start from the main idea, create bullet points, find sources (facts) related to your bullet points, write sentences describing those facts, and write what you have learned. Thinking in this way will help you get unstuck every time.

Writing Heading Paragraphs:
- Introduction paragraph
- Body paragraphs (subheading paragraphs if needed)
- Conclusion paragraph

Writing Subheading Paragraphs:
- Introduction paragraph
- Body paragraphs
- Conclusion paragraph

Writing Paragraphs: Every paragraph must have an introduction sentence, supporting body sentences, and a conclusion. Adding facts to your paragraphs adds richness. A paragraph should be 3 – 12 sentences long.
- Introduction sentence: It explains what you will talk about in your paragraph
- Body sentences: Expands upon the introduction sentence. Uses fact(s) from a reliable source (in-text citation and reference). You can compare the facts. You can stack facts to support one idea. You could even show contradictions from different authors. Then, explain your fact with your own

words. Good body sentences are supportive of your introduction sentence, 2 – 8 sentences long are ideal

- Conclusion sentence: It summarizes all the points you have made and/or introduces the next paragraph.

Writing Sentences: Each sentence must have at least one subject, one verb, and an idea that makes sense. The best sentences are simple sentences. If your sentences are more than 15 words long, cut it, and start a new sentence.

Writing Dissertation Chapters: Write each chapter based on all the headings and subheadings that your university requires. Just write down a few words to describe each heading and subheading. You will have the opportunity within each chapter to write down your university's chapter requirements.

There are tons of other ways to write. Any writing format such as MEAL will help you write like a professional. Whatever format you use, use it to tell a clear story that your audience would enjoy.

2. Select a Survey or Prior Experiment:

Survey:

One of the easiest ways to complete your dissertation is to find a prior study that interest you, use their survey, and redo that study using data that you have collected (called primary data collection). The benefit of using an existing study and survey is that it provides a good template of what survey was selected, what hypothesis test was used, and an explanation of the findings. A possible drawback of using an existing survey is that you will need to get approval to use it. I would highly recommend using an existing survey.

Note: All survey questions and approvals should be documented in Appendix Pages of your dissertation. Select a survey that will help you solves a problem.

A good Survey must be:

- Approximately 40 questions
- A Likert Scale (answers must have 2, 3, 5, or 7 options)
- Used in a journal article, magazine, book, dissertation, etc…
- Developed 20 years or less
- Simple to read, simple to understand, and simple to get approval to use
- Easy to copy and share

Survey Check List		
Survey Name:		
40 questions or less	Yes ☐	No ☐
A Likert Scale	Yes ☐	No ☐
Used in a public source	Yes ☐	No ☐
Developed 10 years or less	Yes ☐	No ☐
Simple: read/understand/approval	Yes ☐	No ☐
Easy to copy/share	Yes ☐	No ☐

Note: You will have to do a Power Analysis to compute the effective sample size minimum you will need for your study (n > 35)

What Power Analysis tool (ex. G*Power 3) will you use?

_____

What sample size will you need? _____

Survey Process:
- Find or develop a survey
- Get approval (Consent Form & Letter of Permission from author & university if applicable)
- Identify which tool you will use to distribute your survey (Ex. Email, SurveyMonkey, mail, etc…)
  - Exclude personal identification questions
  - Include needed identification questions
- Identify how you will notify participants (email, phone calls, face-to-face, etc…)
  - Write Letter of Recruitment
  - Write Acknowledgement Informed Consent Form
  - Write Participant Reminder Email
- Identify how long you will have your survey available (3 to 4 weeks is ideal)

  Note: If you have not attained your calculated sample size, extend your survey time accordingly.

- Setup questions in the distribution tool (Ex. SurveyMonkey, etc…)
  - Include Acknowledgment Informed Consent Form
  - Require all questions to be answered by participants
  - Questions need to be static and fixed
  - Must be anonymous
- Export your data into a statistical tool (Excel, SPSS, etc…)

Note: If you are developing your own survey, ensure that your questions are:
- Validated
- Approximately 40 questions
- A Likert Scale (answers must have 2, 3, 5, or 7 options)

Prior Experiment:
Another way to collect data is by using data collected by another researcher (called secondary data collection). For my initial dissertation, I used secondary data to complete my dissertation within a week. Typically, you should only use secondary data that was collected within a time period of 5 years.

Note: Most researchers who have collected data don't ask all the questions related to the data they have collected. You can look for a gap and write about it in your dissertation.

Prior Experiment Check List		
Prior Experiment Data Collections Name:		
Used in a public source	Yes ☐	No ☐
Developed 5 years or less	Yes ☐	No ☐
Simple: read/understand/approval	Yes ☐	No ☐
Easy to copy/share	Yes ☐	No ☐

3. Choose Your Main Tests:

There are two main types of tests in a quantitative study; descriptive statistics and hypothesis testing. You should use both! You will be able to document the central tendencies within your study and determine if there is a relationship. If you know and understand these main tests and its results, you will be able to have a clear goal that informs your entire dissertation.

Two Main Test:
- Descriptive Statistic
- Hypothesis Test (Choose One):
    - T-Test/Paired T-Test
    - One-Way/Two-Way ANOVA
    - ANCOVA
    - Mann-Whitney U Test
    - Chi-square Test
    - Pearson Product Moment Correlations
    - Linear/Multiple Regression
    - Spearman Rank-Order Correlation

Note: I recommend that you choose a hypothesis test based on the study of the survey or based on a question you would like answered.

Each statistical test will be presented in terms of a framework called DCOVA. It is a process used in statistics to understand and write any statistical test. DCOVA stands for:
- D – Define: You must define the problem and/or question
- C – Collect: Use a Survey or prior experiment to collect data
- O – Organize: Clean and unify data
- V – Visualize: Display your results
- A – Analyze: Document calculations, findings, & interpretations

Here are the descriptions of each test:

Descriptive Statistic:

- Define: You are looking to get information about the Mean, Median, Mode, Standard Error, Standard Deviation, Range, and Sample Size
- Collect: Survey or Prior Experiment
- Organize: Format Data into Tables
- Visualize: Scatter Plot, Pie Chart
- Analyze: Use a statistical tool (Excel, SPSS), insert the Descriptive Statistics output, document, and interpret your results

Excel Example:

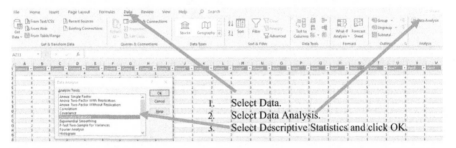

1. Select Data.
2. Select Data Analysis.
3. Select Descriptive Statistics and click OK.

4. Enter the cell range

5. Check the Summary Statistics box

6. Click OK

Output Results

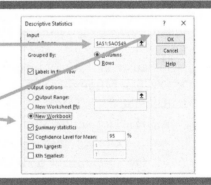

	Comm1		Comm2
Mean	3.25	Mean	2.729167
Standard Error	0.144338	Standard Error	0.156818
Median	3	Median	3
Mode	4	Mode	2
Standard Deviation	1	Standard Deviation	1.086466
Sample Variance	1	Sample Variance	1.180408
Kurtosis	-0.3926	Kurtosis	-0.54499
Skewness	-0.26642	Skewness	0.36407
Range	4	Range	4
Minimum	1	Minimum	1
Maximum	5	Maximum	5
Sum	156	Sum	131
Count	48	Count	48
Confidence Level(95.0%)	0.29037	Confidence Level(95.0%)	0.315477

16

t-test/paired t-test:

- Define:
    - Comparison: Testing single/paired/independent Groups
    - Independent (unrelated) groups – equal/unequal variance t-tests or
    - Dependent (same/related) samples – paired t-test
    - Question: Examine the difference between _____ [(in)dependent variable 1] on _____ [(in)dependent variable 2]
    - H0: There are no significant differences between _____ [(in)dependent variables] on _____ [(in)dependent variable]
    - H1: There are significant differences between _____ [(in)dependent variables] on _____ [(in)dependent variable]
- Collect: Survey or Prior Experiment
- Organize: Format Data into Tables
- Visualize: Box Plot
- Analyze (Interpret): Use a statistical tool (Excel, SPSS) and document your results
    - No, there are no significant differences between _____ [(in)dependent variables] on _____ [(in)dependent variable]
        - If tstat is > (-) tcrit or < (+) tcrit, then do not reject the null hypothesis or
        - If p-value is greater than your level of significance (alpha), then do not reject the null hypothesis (ex. p-value = 0.06 > level of significance = 0.05 Accept)
    - Yes, there are significant differences between _____ [(in)dependent variables] on _____ [(in)dependent variable]

17

- If tstat is < (-) tcrit or > (+) tcrit, then reject the null hypothesis or
- If p-value is less than your alpha (ex. 0.05), then reject the null hypothesis (ex. p-value = 0.04 < level of significance = 0.05 Reject)

Excel Example:

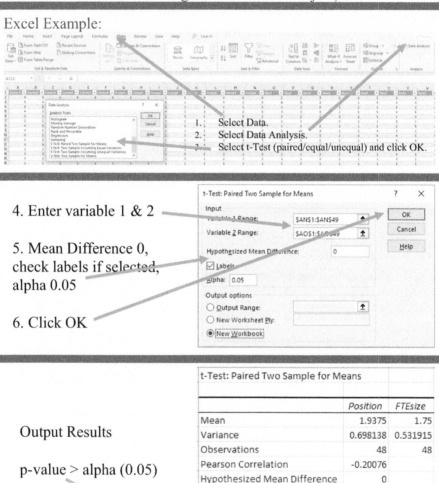

1. Select Data.
2. Select Data Analysis.
3. Select t-Test (paired/equal/unequal) and click OK.

4. Enter variable 1 & 2

5. Mean Difference 0, check labels if selected, alpha 0.05

6. Click OK

Output Results

p-value > alpha (0.05)

Do not reject the Null Hypothesis

t-Test: Paired Two Sample for Means		
	Position	FTEsize
Mean	1.9375	1.75
Variance	0.698138	0.531915
Observations	48	48
Pearson Correlation	-0.20076	
Hypothesized Mean Difference	0	
df	47	
t Stat	1.069707	
P(T<=t) one-tail	0.145107	
t Critical one-tail	1.677927	
P(T<=t) two-tail	0.290214	
t Critical two-tail	2.011741	

One-Way/Two-Way ANOVA:
- Define:
    - Comparison: Test Independent Variable(s) on Dependent Variable (sample size the same)
    - Independent (unrelated) Variable(s): 1 or more
    - Dependent (related) Variable: 1
    - Question: A research study was conducted to examine _____ (dependent variable) on _____ (independent variable)
    - H0: There will be no difference in _____ (dependent variable) on _____ (independent variable)
    - H1: There will be a difference in _____ (dependent variable) on _____ (independent variable)
- Collect: Survey or Prior Experiment
- Organize: Format Data into Tables
- Visualize: Plot (mean, interactive, scatter)
- Analyze (Interpret): Use a statistical tool (Excel, SPSS) & document your results
    - No, there is no difference in _____ (dependent variable) on _____ (independent variable)
        - If Fstat is < Fcrit value, then do not reject the null hypothesis or
        - If your one-tail p-value is greater than your level of significance (alpha), then do not reject the null hypothesis (ex. p-value = 0.06 > alpha = 0.05 Accept)
    - Yes, there is a significant difference in _____ (dependent variable) on _____ (independent variable) [Fstat = _____ and p _____ (< or >)]
        - If Fstat is > Fcrit, then reject the null hypothesis or
        - If your one-tail p-value is less than your level of significance (ex. 0.05), then reject the null

19

hypothesis (ex. p-value = 0.04 < alpha = 0.05
Reject)

Excel Example:

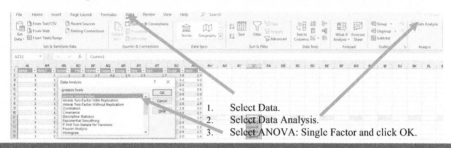

1. Select Data.
2. Select Data Analysis.
3. Select ANOVA: Single Factor and click OK.

4. Enter dependent and
independent variables

5. Check labels if selected
and alpha 0.05

6. Click OK

Anova: Single Factor

Input Range: SAMS1:SANS49

Grouped By: ● Columns ○ Rows

☑ Labels in first row
Alpha: 0.05

Output options
○ Output Range:
○ New Worksheet Ply:
● New Workbook

OK
Cancel
Help

Anova: Single Factor

SUMMARY

Groups	Count	Sum	Average	Variance
Skills7	48	103	2.145833	0.935727
Position	48	93	1.9375	0.698138

ANOVA

Source of Variation	SS	df	MS	F	P-value	F crit
Between Groups	1.041667	1	1.041667	1.275095	0.261687	3.942303
Within Groups	76.79167	94	0.816933			
Total	77.83333	95				

Output Results: p-value > alpha (0.05) then do not reject Null Hypothesis

20

Analysis of Covariances (ANCOVA):
- Define:
    - Comparison: Group
    - Independent Variable(s): 1 or more
    - Dependent Variable(s): 1
    - Controlled Variable: 1 Covariance
    - Question: Determine the effects of the _____ (independent variable) on the _____ (dependent variable) adjusted for the presence of _____ (covariance(s)) in the model
    - H0: There is no significant effect of the _____ (independent variable) on the _____ (dependent variable) controlling for _____ (covariance(s)) in the model
    - H1: There is a significant effect of the _____ (independent variable) on the _____ (dependent variable) controlling for _____ (covariance(s)) in the model
- Collect: Survey or Prior Experiment
- Organize: Format Data into Tables
- Visualize: Scatter Plot
- Analyze (Interpret): Use a statistical tool (Excel, SPSS) & document your results
    - No, there is no difference in _____ (dependent variable) on _____ (independent variable)
        - If Fstat is < Fcrit value, then do not reject the null hypothesis or
        - If your one-tail p-value is greater than your level of significance, then do not reject the null hypothesis (ex. p-value = 0.06 > level of significance = 0.05 Accept)
    - Yes, there is a significant difference in _____ (dependent variable) on _____ (independent variable) [Fstat = ___ and p ___ (< or >)]

21

- If Fstat is > Fcrit, then reject the null hypothesis
  or
- If your one-tail p-value is less than your level of significance (ex. 0.05), then reject the null hypothesis (ex. p-value = 0.04 < level of significance = 0.05 Reject)

Excel Example: Not simple to calculate

Mann-Whitney U Test:

- Define:
  - Comparison: Samples
  - Sample 1: _____ (Name)
  - Sample 2: _____ (Name)
  - Question: Determine the difference between sample 1 and sample
  - H0: There is no significant difference in _____ (Sample 1) and _____ (Sample 2)
  - H1: There is a significant difference in _____ (Sample 1) and _____ (Sample 2)
- Collect: Survey or Prior Experiment
- Organize: Format Data into Tables
- Visualize: Box Plot
- Analyze (Interpret): Use a statistical tool (Excel, SPSS) & document your results
  - Excel:
  - No, there is no significant difference in _____ (Sample 1) and _____ (Sample 2)
  - Yes, there is a significant difference in _____ (Sample 1) and _____ (Sample 2) [Improve or Address]

Excel Example: Not simple to calculate

Chi-square Test:
- Define:
    - Comparison: Association between Groups (proportions – contingency table)
    - Group 1 & 2: Subgroups (2x2 table: testing proportions)
    - Group 1 & 2: Subgroups (3^+x3^+ table: testing independence)
    - Question: Is there evidence that group 1 is equal or independent of the proportion of group 2?
    - H0: _____ (Group 1) and _____ (Group 2) are equal or independent
    - H1: The two proportions are not the same or dependent
- Collect: Survey or Prior Experiment
- Organize: Format Data into Tables
- Visualize: Plot (Mosaic)
- Analyze (Interpret): Use a statistical tool (Excel, SPSS) & document your results
    - Excel: p-value CHITEST(actual_range,expected_range)
    - No, _____ (Group 1) and _____ (Group 2) are equal or independent
        - If X^2stat is < X^2crit value, then do not reject the null hypothesis or
        - If your one-tail p-value is greater than your level of significance (alpha), then do not reject the null hypothesis (ex. p-value = 0.06 > alpha = 0.05 Accept)
    - Yes, the two proportions are not the same or dependent
        - If X^2stat is > X^2crit, then reject the null hypothesis or
        - If your one-tail p-value is less than your alpha (ex. 0.05), then reject the null hypothesis (ex. p-value = 0.04 < alpha = 0.05 Reject)

24

Excel Example:

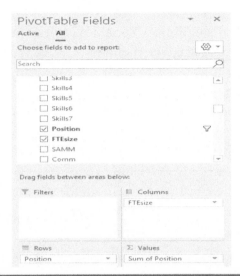

	A	B	C	D	E
1	**Sum of Position**	**Column Labels** ▼			
2	**Row Labels** ⌕		**Small**	**Medium**	**Large** **Grand Total**
3	Leaders		4	12	2	18
4	Directors		14	8	8	30
5	Top Managers		27	12	6	45
6	**Grand Total**		**45**	**32**	**16**	**93**
7					
8					
9				fe = row total x column total/sample size
10			8.71=(18*45)/93		
11					
12	Expected		Small	Medium	Large	Total
13	Leaders		8.71	6.19	3.10	18
14	Directors		14.52	10.32	5.16	30
15	Top Managers		21.77	15.48	7.74	45
16	Total		45	32	16	93
17					
18	p-value	CHITEST(B3:E6,B13:E16)		0.17 > 0.05	
19	Therefore we would accept the null hypothesis (independent)				

Output Results

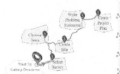

Pearson Product Moment Correlation:
- Define:
    - o Comparison: Relate Variables (note: you can also use Pearson to make predictions)
    - o Variable 1: _____ (Name)
    - o Variable 2: _____ (Name)
    - o Question: Is there evidence of a relationship between _____ (variable 1) and _____ (variable 2)
    - o H0: There is no statistically significant relationship between _____ (variable 1) and _____ (variable 2)
    - o H1: There is a statistically significant relationship between _____ (variable 1) and _____ (variable 2)
- Collect: Survey or Prior Experiment
- Organize: Format Data into Tables
- Visualize: Scatter Plot, Box Plot
- Analyze (Interpret): Use a statistical tool (Excel, SPSS) & document your results
    - o Excel: PEARSON(A2:A31,B2:B31)
    - o No, there is no statistically significant relationship between _____ (variable 1) and _____ (variable 2)
        - ▪ If correl (r) = 0, no correlation
    - o Yes, there is a weak negative statistically significant relationship between _____ (variable 1) and _____ (variable 2)
        - ▪ If correl (r) = -0.3, weak negative correlation
    - o Yes, there is a strong negative statistically significant relationship between _____ (variable 1) and _____ (variable 2)
        - ▪ If correl (r) = -1, strong negative correlation
    - o Yes, there is a weak positive statistically significant relationship between _____ (variable 1) and _____ (variable 2)
        - ▪ If correl (r) = 0.3, weak positive correlation

- o Yes, there is a strong positive statistically significant relationship between _____ (variable 1) and _____ (variable 2)
    - If correl (r) = 1, strong positive correlation

Excel Example: Perform a Pearson correlation between two columns. Pearson correlation (r) is between -1 and 1. Negative 1 is a strong negative correlation and posssitive 1 is a strong possitive correlation.

In Excel enter: =PEARSON(Column1,Column2)
                        =PEARSON(A2:A31,B2:B31)

Note: Don't include the labels in your formula of each column

Linear/Multiple Regression Analysis:
- Define:
  - Comparison: Relate Variables
  - Independent Variable(s){x}: 1 or more
  - Dependent Variable(s){y}: 1
  - Question: Determine the predictive power of one or more independent variable on a dependent variable
  - H0: There is no significant prediction of _____ (dependent variable) by _____ (independent variable 1), and/or _____ (independent variable 2), and/or _____ (etc…)
  - H1: There is a significant prediction of _____ (dependent variable) by _____ (independent variable 1), and/or _____ (independent variable 2), and/or _____ (etc…)
- Collect: Survey or Prior Experiment
- Organize: Format Data into Tables
- Visualize: Scatter Plot, Regression Output
- Analyze (Interpret): Use a statistical tool (Excel, SPSS) & document your results
  - Excel: Data Analysis – Regression
  - No, there is no significant prediction of _____ (dependent variable) by _____ (independent variable 1), and/or _____ (independent variable 2), and/or _____ (etc…)
    - If Fstat is < Fcrit value, then do not reject the null hypothesis or
    - If your one-tail p-value is greater than your level of significance, then do not reject the null hypothesis (ex. p-value = 0.06 > level of significance = 0.05 Accept)
  - Yes, there is a significant prediction of _____ (dependent variable) by _____ (independent variable 1), and/or _____ (independent variable 2), and/or _____ (etc…) [Fstat = ___ and p ___ (< or >)]

28

- If Fstat is > Fcrit, then reject the null hypothesis or
- If your one-tail p-value is less than your level of significance (ex. 0.05), then reject the null hypothesis (ex. p-value = 0.04 < level of significance = 0.05 Reject)

Excel Example:

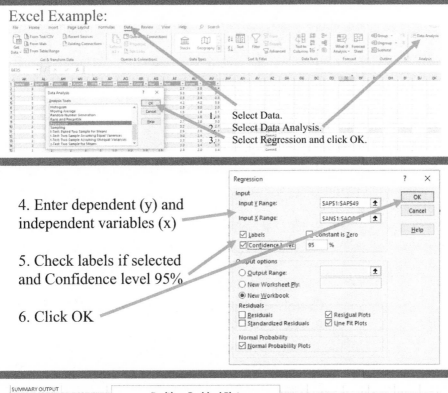

1. Select Data.
2. Select Data Analysis.
3. Select Regression and click OK.

4. Enter dependent (y) and independent variables (x)

5. Check labels if selected and Confidence level 95%

6. Click OK

SUMMARY OUTPUT

Regression Statistics	
Multiple R	0.068396982
R Square	0.004678147
Adjusted R Square	-0.03955838
Standard Error	0.668528398
Observations	48

ANOVA

	df	SS	MS	F	Significance F
Regression	2	0.094528459	0.047264	0.105753	0.899869713
Residual	45	20.11185988	0.44693		
Total	47	20.20638834			

	Coefficients	Standard Error	t Stat	P-value	Lower 95%	Upper 95%	Lower 95.0%	Upper 95.0%
Intercept	2.655587312	0.376527765	7.052814	8.51E-09	1.89721945	3.413955173	1.89721945	3.413955173
Position	-0.042748614	0.119133398	-0.35883	0.721401	-0.282695595	0.197198367	-0.282695595	0.197198367
FTEsize	-0.04829372	0.136484454	-0.35384	0.725111	-0.323187521	0.226600081	-0.323187521	0.226600081

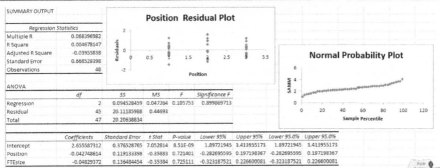

29

Spearman Rank-Order Correlation:

- Define:
    - Comparison: Relate Ranked Variables
    - Rank 1: _____ (Name)
    - Rank 2: _____ (Name)
    - Question: Determine the relationship between _____ (Rank 1) and _____ (Rank 2)
    - H0: There is no relationship between _____ (Rank 1) and _____ (Rank 2)
    - H1: There is a relationship between _____ (Rank 1) and _____ (Rank 2)
- Collect: Survey or Prior Experiment
- Organize: Format Data into Tables
- Visualize: Scatter Plot, Box Plot
- Analyze (Interpret): Use a statistical tool (Excel, SPSS) & document your results
    - Excel:
        - Rank 1: RANK(A2,$A$2:$A$31,1) place answers where applicable
        - Rank 2: RANK(B2,$B$2:$B$31,1) place answers where applicable
        - Correlation Formula: PEARSON(C2:C31,D2:D31)
    - No, there is no statistically significant relationship between _____ (Rank 1) and _____ (Rank 2)
        - If correl (r) = 0, no correlation
    - Yes, there is a weak negative statistically significant relationship between _____ (Rank 1) and _____ (Rank 2)
        - If correl (r) = -0.3, weak negative correlation
    - Yes, there is a strong negative statistically significant relationship between _____ (Rank 1) and _____ (Rank 2)
        - If correl (r) = -1, strong negative correlation

- Yes, there is a weak positive statistically significant relationship between _____ (Rank 1) and _____ (Rank 2)
  - If correl (r) = 0.3, weak positive correlation
- Yes, there is a strong positive statistically significant relationship between _____ (Rank 1) and _____ (Rank 2)
  - If correl (r) = 1, strong positive correlation

Excel Example: Perform a Ranked correlation between two columns. Ranked correlation (r) is between -1 and 1. Negative 1 is a strong negative correlation and positive 1 is a strong positive correlation.

First: Rank each column
In Excel enter:
- Rank 1: RANK(A2,$A$2:$A$31,1) place answers where applicable
  = RANK(A2,$A$2:$A$31,1)
- Rank 2: RANK(B2,$B$2:$B$31,1) place answers where applicable
  = RANK(B2,$B$2:$B$31,1)

Second: Conduct a PEARSON Correlation
In Excel enter: =PEARSON(Column1,Column2)
                       =PEARSON(A2:A31,B2:B31)

Note: Don't include the labels in your formula of each column

31

Choose your hypothesis test:

Which hypothesis test did you choose? _____

What is the question related to your test?

_____

_____

_____

What are your hypothesis questions?

$H0$:_____

_____

$H1$:_____

_____

Will you ask any subtopic hypothesis questions? If so, what are they?

$H0_1$:_____

_____

$H1_1$:_____

_____

$H0_2$:_____

_____

$H1_2$:_____

_____

$H0_3$:_____

_____

$H1_3$:_____

_____   _____

After you have chosen your hypothesis test, you want to create your title and develop your problem statement. Your title and problem statement will be easy to construct because it directly links to the survey and hypothesis test in which you have chosen. Your title should be simple, no more than 20 words, and quantitative. Your problem statement should also be simple, precise, and clear. Let the writing begin

4. **Create Your Title:**
   - Must be related to the survey and hypothesis test of your choosing
   - Must be limited to 20 words or less
   - Must include main variables
   - Must include the area of study

Here is an example of my title:
"Assessing Information Technology and Business Alignment in Local City Government Agencies"

Write your title here:

_____
_____
_____

5. Writing Your Problem Statement:
- Find three sources that address your problem statement
- Identify the lack of information related to your study based on existing research
- State the problem your study seeks to address (must be related to the survey and hypothesis test of your choosing)
- State the goal of your study

Here is an example of my Problem Statement:

Problem Statement

Aligning IT and business is a crucial issue for IT executives (Khaiata & Zualkernan, 2009). Chen (2010) noted that the number one concern of IT management and business executives is to understand how IT and business align. Luftman, Ben-Zvi, Dwivedi, and Rigoni (2010) have collected a benchmark repository of over 2,000 organizations measuring IT/business alignment using the SAMM instrument. Only one organization out of 2,000 agencies within Luftman's benchmark repository was a government agency. The problem my study sought to address was the lack of information regarding LCGAs IT/business strategic alignment maturity level and its employment size. The goal of this study was to understand how a city's strategic alignment maturity level might affect large, medium, and small city employment size and to understand its current maturity level.

Write your Problem Statement:

_____
_____
_____
_____
_____
_____
_____
_____
_____
_____
_____

6. Project Plan:

Create a Project Plan: Approach your dissertation like it is a project that you must complete within a realistic timeline. Follow your project plan as best as you can. Look at each section and determine how long you would like to spend on it. Try your best to stick to your timeline. Present your timeline to God and He will make your path straight. Adjust it accordingly! Table 1 is a basic project plan that you and/or your dissertation committee members agree to and can use. Get their buy-in and get it done!

Sections	Completion Date	Completed (Y/N)
Get Directions: Write Down Your University's Dissertation Heading Requirements		
Select a Survey or prior experiment		
Choose a Hypothesis Test		
Create a Title		
Write your Problem Statement		
Complete Chapter 1		
Complete Chapter 2		
Complete Chapter 3		
Complete Data Collection		
Complete Chapter 4		
Complete Chapter 5		
References Page		
Appendix Pages		
Title Page		
Abstract Page		
Dedication Page		
Acknowledgment Page		
Table of Contents Page		
List of Tables		
List of Figures		

Table 1: Write Your Project Plan

36

Summary

The quantitative dissertation process is simple once you understand it holistically. If you don't know where to start and how to build a solid foundation, you will be just as confused and frustrated like I was at the beginning of my dissertation process. If you have a good starting point, your entire dissertation will be easy to write.

Starting Point:
1. Get Directions: Write down your university's dissertation heading requirements
2. Select a survey or prior experiment
3. Choose your main test
4. Create a title
5. Write your problem statement
6. Create a project plan

Now that you have a solid foundation, you can go to the next step of completing Chapter 1.

Writing Chapters

Chapter 1

Introduction to the Study

Take some time to submit Chapter 1 to God!

Proverbs 3:6 (NIV) in all your ways submit to him, and he will make your paths straight.

Chapter 1: Introduction to the Study

This is the chapter that sets the foundation for your entire dissertation. You must first understand and list all your University's heading and subheading requirements for this chapter. Write it down and start the process of developing your Chapter 1. Remember, for each heading and subheadings you should always write in terms of the introduction, body, and conclusion paragraphs.

Below is a list of my Chapter 1 heading and subheading requirements:

Get Directions: Write down your University's Chapter 1 heading and
subheading requirements:

Chapter 1: _____

_____
_____
_____
_____
_____
_____
_____
_____
_____
_____
_____
_____
_____
_____
_____
_____
_____
_____
_____
_____
_____
_____
_____
_____
_____
_____
_____
_____
_____
_____

Chapter 1 Introduction (1 – 3 paragraphs):

- Start off your chapter with two or more facts (in-text citations and references) from the main sources of your dissertation. These sources should inform the two areas that you want to assess in your title.
- Your concluding paragraph must list all the areas Chapter 1 will cover.

Background of the Study (~20 paragraph):

- Heading (1 paragraph): Introduction
- Subheading 1: Write about your industry sector
- Subheading 2: Write about your first area to assess
- Subheading 3: Write about your second area to assess
- Heading 4: Summary

Problem Statement (1 paragraph): Insert your problem statement here.

Purpose of the Study (1 – 3 paragraphs): You want to identify your research method as a quantitative survey study. Provide a general location where this study is being conducted (ex. southwestern part of the United States). Use facts to support the survey (instrument) you have used. Identify your variables. Lastly, state how those variables affect the outcome.

Research Question (1 paragraph): Write two or more sentences briefly explaining your research question or problem statement. Here is an example of my research question based on a Linear/Multiple Regression Analysis

> ### Research Question
>
> The research question organizing this study was: What was the relationship between a city's IT/business strategic alignment maturity level and its employment size?
>
> The hypotheses associated with this question were:

List Hypotheses:
- $H0_1$: There is no significant prediction of _____ (dependent variable) by _____ (independent variable 1), and/or _____ (independent variable 2), and/or _____ (etc...)
- $H1_1$: There is a significant prediction of _____ (dependent variable) by _____ (independent variable 1), and/or _____ (independent variable 2), and/or _____ (etc...)

Research Question Subtopics (1 – 6 if applicable)
- $H0_2$: There is no significant prediction of _____ (dependent variable) by _____ (independent variable 1)
- $H1_2$: There is a significant prediction of _____ (dependent variable) by _____ (independent variable 1)
- $H0_3$: There is no significant prediction of _____ (dependent variable) by _____ (independent variable 2)
- $H1_3$: There is a significant prediction of _____ (dependent variable) by _____ (independent variable 2)
- Etc...

Write your research question(s):

_____

_____

_____

_____

List Your Hypothesis:
- $H0_1$: _____

    _____

    _____

- $H1_1$: _____

    _____

    _____

Research Question Subtopics (1 – 6 if applicable):

- HO_2: _____
  _____
  _____
  _____

- $H1_2$: _____
  _____
  _____
  _____

- HO_3: _____
  _____
  _____
  _____

- $H1_3$: _____
  _____
  _____
  _____

Theoretical Framework (3 – 5 paragraphs):
- 1st paragraph: Introduction
  - The theoretical framework for this study is based on Dependent Variable and the instrument used
  - Dependent Variable forms the framework
  - Describe where prior literature was conducted
  - Describe what are your study will look at
- 2nd & 3rd paragraphs: What are sources saying about your different variables?
- 4th paragraph: What are sources saying about your instrument?
- 5th paragraph: What are sources saying about the limited knowledge in your specific study
- 6th paragraph: Conclusion

Nature of the Study (3 paragraphs):
- 1st paragraph: Introduction
  - Quantitative online survey to test hypotheses

- o Find sources that support quantitative surveys as it relates to the population
  - o Conclude by writing about your target population
- 2nd paragraph: Write about online surveys and how you will use it to target your different participants
- 3rd paragraph: Conclude with how you will analyze your data (Excel, SPSS, etc…)

Definition of Terms (10 to 30 defined words): Below is my list:

Definition of Terms

Throughout this study, I identify literature precise words, phrases, and studies that need clarity. Below is a list of terms defined for clarity:

Business strategy: is the overall organizational strategy of LCGAs. This strategy should always be constant in its subcategories or parts but unique to each organization. A metaphor of this concept is the body. It is made up of many different parts such as the head, nose, lips, and ears. No head, nose, lips, or ears are exactly the same. They are all unique. Similarly, business strategy must be constant in subcategory or parts but unique to each organization.

CobiT: A methodology used by organizations to comply with SOX. CobiT is a model for IT management that consist of internal controls and holistic operations controls (Hong, Chi, Chao, & Tang, 2003).

FTEsize: Full-time employment size is the independent variable grouped into three categories; small, medium, and large.

Global Status Report on the Governance of Enterprise IT (GEIT): A 2011 study uses to measure ITG maturity level.

Governance: According to Palczewska, Fu, Trundle, and Yang (2013), governance is a collection of strategies and processes that formally manages problems. I used governance in a similar manner in this study.

List your Definition of Terms:

- _____
- _____
- _____
- _____
- _____
- _____
- _____
- _____
- _____
- _____
- _____
- _____

Assumptions (1 paragraph with 6 assumptions):
- Independent variable wants to understand dependent variable
- Variables are adequate to examine your problem statement
- Your sample is a good representation of the population
- Assumed that the instrument was adequate
- Learn new information about your study

Write Your Assumptions:

- _____
- _____
- _____
- _____
- _____
- _____
- _____
- _____
- _____
- _____

Limitations (1 paragraph with a list of ~5 items): Here is my example:

Limitations

There are limitations in every study. For this study, factors not considered in this design could potentially change the conclusions drawn. This study's limitations include:

1. Data were collected and analyzed from a web survey. Original data were collected using proper research procedures.

2. Data retrieval for the dataset came from SurveyMonkey. Variables are static and fixed.

3. While the sample size may be appropriate for this study, it may not be accurate represent all LCGAs across the U.S.

4. There are also unknown variables not covered that may affect the outcome of the survey.

5. Limited knowledge of IT/business alignment could alter the result of this study

Scope and Delimitations (1 paragraph):
- Define your population based on limitations and boundaries
- It was limited to… (the types of participant)
- Data was collected (online only or by email or mail)
- Independent variable was located where (southwestern region)
- Participants completed the survey on a volunteer basis only

Significance of the Study (~5 paragraphs):
- Heading 1st paragraph: Introduction
- Subheading 1 2nd paragraph: Significance to Theory
- Subheading 2 3rd paragraph: Significance to Practice
- Subheading 3 4th paragraph: Significance of Social Change
- Heading 5th paragraph: Summary

Chapter 1 Summary (~3 paragraphs):
- 1st paragraph: Introduction (Importance of this study to the community)
- 2nd paragraph: Call for action
- 3rd paragraph: Introduce your chapters

Chapter 2

Literature Review

Take some time to submit Chapter 2 to God!

Proverbs 3:6 (NIV) In all your ways submit to him, and he will make your paths straight.

Chapter 2: Literature Review

This chapter describes the history behind your title. Explain the past, current, and evolving literature using facts (reliable sources). You must understand and list all your University's requirements for this chapter. Write it down and start the process of developing your Chapter 2. Remember for each heading and subheadings you should always write in terms of the introduction, body, and conclusion paragraphs. Show how the past and current literature informs your study.

Below is a list of my University's Chapter 2 requirements:

Get Directions: Write down your University's Chapter 2 heading and subheading requirements:
Chapter 2: _____

_____
_____
_____
_____
_____
_____
_____
_____
_____
_____
_____
_____
_____
_____
_____
_____
_____
_____
_____
_____
_____
_____
_____
_____
_____
_____
_____
_____
_____
_____
_____
_____

Chapter 2 Introduction (~3 paragraphs):
- 1st paragraph: Introduction – Use your problem statement to build a case for your literature review
- 2nd paragraph: Explain the main theories that inform your study and briefly describe the history of your study
- 3rd paragraph: Introduce your main headings of this chapter

Search Strategy (2 – 3 paragraphs):
- Describe where you will find your facts from (ex. eBooks, journal articles, online links, & libraries)
- Describe how these sources will inform your study
- List keyword searches (ex. ITG, ITIL, ITSM, MIS, etc…)

Theoretical Foundation (7+ pages)
- Heading: Introduction (3+ paragraphs)
- Subheading 1 (3+ paragraphs):
- Subheading 2 (3+ paragraphs):
- Subheading 3 (3+ paragraphs):
- Conclusion (1 – 3 paragraphs)

Literature Review (15+ pages)
- Heading: Introduction (~3 paragraphs)
- Subheading 1 (3+ paragraphs): History of your topic
- Subheading 2 (3+ paragraphs): Current literature researched for area 1
- Subheading 3 (3+ paragraphs): Popular methodology for area 1
- Subheading 4 (3+ paragraphs): Current literature researched for area 2
- Subheading 5 (3+ paragraphs): Current literature researched for industry sector
- Subheading 6 (3+ paragraphs): Literature and research-based analysis (ex. the importance of alignment)

- Subheading 7 (10+ paragraphs): Present Study - Find sources that write about current aspects of your topic and the conclusions they made
- Subheading 8 (3+ paragraphs): Rationale – Show how the literature explains the rationale behind your study
- Conclusion (1 – 3 paragraphs)

Chapter 2 Summary and Conclusions (1 – 3 paragraphs):
- Recap what you have covered in this chapter
- Identify noteworthy sources
- Introduce the next chapter

Chapter 3

Research
Method

Take some time to submit Chapter 3 to God!

Proverbs 3:6 (NIV) In all your ways submit to him, and he will make your paths straight.

Chapter 3: Research Method

This chapter describes your research method. Restate your purpose statement and describe each element of your research method. You must understand and list all your University's requirements for this chapter. Write it down and start the process of developing your chapter 3. Remember for each heading and subheadings you should always write in terms of the introduction, body, and conclusion paragraphs. Your research method must describe your inquiry methods found in Starting Point 2 and 3 (select survey & choose tests).

Below is a list of my Chapter 3 requirements:

55

Get Directions: Write down your University's Chapter 3 heading and subheading requirements:

Chapter 3: _____

_____

_____

_____

_____

_____

_____

_____

_____

_____

_____

_____

_____

_____

_____

_____

_____

_____

_____

_____

_____

_____

_____

_____

_____

_____

_____

_____

_____

_____

_____

_____

Chapter 3 Introduction (~3 paragraphs):
- 1st paragraph: Introduction – Use your problem statement to describe the purpose of your quantitative survey study
- 2nd paragraph: Briefly describe what previous studies have investigated
- 3rd paragraph: Introduce your main headings of this chapter

Research Design and Rationale (~5 paragraphs):
- 1st paragraph: Introduction - Explain the rationale for choosing a quantitative nonexperimental study design
- 2nd paragraph: Briefly describe Topic A's dependent variables and insert a table briefly explaining your sub-variables
- 3rd paragraph: Briefly describe Topic B's independent variable and explain your sub-variables
- 4th paragraph: Identify sources that link Topic A & B to alignment
- 5th paragraph: Conclusion

Methodology (~5 paragraphs): Quantitative
- 1st paragraph: Introduction – Describe each method and explain why you chose a quantitative method
- 2nd paragraph: Describe 3 or more sources that have used a quantitative method that relates to your study
- 3rd paragraph: Describe areas that researchers have said need more quantitative exploration
- 4th paragraph: Describe your design method, nonexperimental design
- 5th paragraph: Introduce subheading topics such as population, sampling procedures, recruitment/participation/data collection, instrument, dependent variables, and independent variables
  - Population: 1 paragraph
  - Sampling Procedures: 5+ paragraphs (must calculate your appropriate sampling size – G*Power 3 Tool)

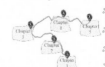

- o Recruitment/Participation/Data Collection: 1 – 5 paragraphs
- o Instrument & Operationalization of Construct: 3 paragraphs
- o Dependent Variables: 1 – 6 paragraphs
- o Independent Variables: 1 – 3 paragraphs

Data Analysis (~4 paragraphs):
- 1st paragraph: Introduction – Introduce your analysis tool (SPSS, Excel, etc…) and the type of analysis test you used
- 2nd paragraph: Rewrite your Hypotheses
- 3rd paragraph: Describe your analysis test
- 4th paragraph: Conclusion

Threats to Validity
- 1st paragraph: Introduction
- 2nd paragraph: External Validity (applying study to population)
- 3rd paragraph: Internal Validity (validating your instrument)
- 4th paragraph: Construct Validity (Instrument presentation bias)
- 5th – 8th paragraphs: Ethical Procedures – APA/MLA standards, confidentiality, consent, organization approvals, dissertation committee members approvals, and IRB approvals
- 6th paragraph: Conclusion

Chapter 3 Summary (1 – 3 paragraphs):
- Recap what you have covered in this chapter
- Restate why your research method is appropriate
- Introduce the next chapter

Chapter 4

Results

Take some time to submit Chapter 4 to God!

Proverbs 3:6 (NIV) in all your ways submit to him, and he will make your paths straight.

Chapter 4: Results

This chapter describes your findings and results from your survey or prior experiment. You must understand and list all your University's requirements for this chapter. Write it down and start the process of developing your chapter. Remember for each heading and subheadings you should always write in terms of the introduction, body, and conclusion paragraphs. Show and display the data you have collected.

Below is a list of my Chapter 4 requirements:

Get Directions: Write down your University's Chapter 4 heading and subheading requirements:

Chapter 4: _____

_____

_____

_____

_____

_____

_____

_____

_____

_____

_____

_____

_____

_____

_____

_____

_____

_____

_____

_____

_____

_____

_____

_____

_____

_____

_____

_____

_____

_____

_____

_____

Chapter 4 Introduction (~3 paragraphs):
- 1st paragraph: Introduction – Findings and results
- 2nd paragraph: Snapshot of the current environment
- 3rd paragraph: Introduce your main headings of this chapter

Data Collection (~10 pages):
- 1st paragraph: Introduction – Introduce your plan/time frame, discrepancies, and descriptive statistics
- Subheading 1: Plan/Time Frame
  - Document your original survey collection plan (List)
  - Document all that happened during your open survey period
- Subheading 2: Discrepancies
  - Document your actual survey collection experience (List)
  - Document any other discrepancy you may have found
- Subheading 3: Descriptive Statistics – Describe it and include all graphs and charts
- Conclusion

Results (~10 pages):
- Introduction paragraph: Restate your problem statement
- Paragraphs: Number based on your research questions (descriptive statistics & test results)
  - Write about your descriptive statistics
  - Display your descriptive statistics
  - Write about your hypothesis test results
  - Display your hypothesis test results (ex. charts, graphs, plots, etc…)
- Conclusion paragraph: Recap your results

Chapter 4 Summary (1 – 3 paragraphs):
- Recap what you have covered in this chapter
- Restate your findings and results
- Introduce the next chapter

Chapter 5

Conclusions & Recommendations

Take some time to submit this final chapter to God!

Proverbs 3:6 (NIV) In all your ways submit to him, and he will make your paths straight.

Chapter 5: Conclusions & Recommendations

This chapter provides discussions, conclusions, and recommendations for future studies. The goal is to tie everything together. You must understand and list all your University's requirements for this chapter. Write it down and start the process of developing your chapter. Remember for each heading and subheadings you should always write in terms of the introduction, body, and conclusion paragraphs. Interpret your results from Chapter 4 and make recommendations for the future.

Below is a list of my Chapter 5 requirements:

Get Directions: Write down your University's Chapter 5 heading and
subheading requirements:
Chapter 5: _____

_____

_____

_____

_____

_____

_____

_____

_____

_____

_____

_____

_____

_____

_____

_____

_____

_____

_____

_____

_____

_____

_____

_____

_____

_____

_____

_____

_____

_____

_____

Chapter 5 Introduction (~3 paragraphs):
- 1st paragraph: Introduction – Purpose statement
- 2nd paragraph: Connect Chapters 1, 2, 3, & 4
- 3rd paragraph: Introduce your main headings of this chapter

Interpretation (~4 pages):
- Introduction paragraph: Introduce your main findings
- Paragraphs: Focus on your descriptive statistics, and the hypothesis test results
  - Write about the survey
  - Write the interpretation of your findings based on your descriptive statistics
  - Write the interpretation of your findings based on your hypothesis test results
- Conclusion paragraph: Recap your findings by focusing on the importance of the finding to your target audience

Limitations (~6 paragraphs):
- 1st paragraph: Introduction
- 2nd paragraph: Sample size
- 3rd paragraph: Area of coverage
- 4th paragraph: Personal interactions with participants
- 5th paragraph: Time needed to take the survey
- 6th paragraph: Recap limitations

Recommendations (~6 paragraphs):
- 1st paragraph: Introduction
- 2nd paragraph: Descriptive statistics
- 3rd paragraph: Hypothesis test results
- 4th paragraph: Write about the next survey level and the benefits of the next survey level
- 5th paragraph: State your recommendations on what other studies should address
- 6th paragraph: Recap recommendations

Implications (~4 paragraphs):
- 1st paragraph: Introduction – The current and future state
- 2nd paragraph: Need to evaluate the current state
- 3rd paragraph: How to attain a future state
- 4th paragraph: Recap of decision-making implications

Chapter 5 Summary (1 – 3 paragraphs):
- Recap what you have covered in this chapter
- Restate your conclusions, recommendations & Implications
- Challenge your audience to improve

Complete Pages

References Page

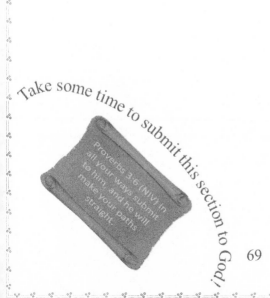

Take some time to submit this section to God!

Proverbs 3:6 (NIV) in all your ways submit to him, and he will make your paths straight.

References Page

Write down all your references. You should aim for approximately 75+ references. Below is a snapshot of my references page:

References

Abels, M. (2014). Strategic alignment for the new normal collaboration, sustainability, and deliberation in local government across boundaries. *State and Local Government Review, 46*(3), 11-218. doi:10.1177/0160323X14551179

Abu-Musa, A. (2009). Exploring the importance and implementation of COBIT processes in Saudi organizations: An empirical study. *Information Management & Computer Security, 17*(2), 73-95. doi:10.1108/09685220910963974

Alcott, L. (2008). *IT governance maturity and context* (ECAR Research Study 5). Retrieved from the Educause Center for Applied Research website: http://net .educause.edu/ir/library/pdf/ers0805/rs/ers08053.pdf

Ali, S., & Green, P. (2012). Effective information technology (IT) governance mechanisms: An IT outsourcing perspective. *Information Systems Frontiers, 14*(2), 179-193. doi:10.1007/s10796-009-9183-y

Allen, B., & Boynton, A. (1991). Information architecture: In search of efficient flexibility. *MIS Quarterly, 15*(4), 435-445. doi:10.2307/249447

Alsudiri, T., Al-Karaghouli, W., & Eldabi, T. (2013). Alignment of large project management process to business strategy: A review and conceptual framework. *Journal of Enterprise Information Management, 26*(5), 596-615. doi:10.1108 /JEIM-07-2013-0050

Avison, D., Jones, J., Powell, P., & Wilson, D. (2002). Using and validating the strategic alignment model. *Journal of Strategic Information Systems, 13*(2004), 223-246. doi:10.1016/j.jsis.2004.08.002

Complete Pages

Appendix
Pages

Take some time to submit this section to God!

Proverbs 3:6 (NIV) In all your ways submit to him, and he will make your paths straight.

Appendix Pages

You should have at least 5 or more separate appendix sections. Below is an example of my appendix list and appendixes.

Write your Appendix list:

_____

_____

_____

_____

_____

_____

_____

_____

_____

_____

Complete Pages

Appendix A: Consent Forms

Title:	Business–IT alignment maturity of companies in China
Author:	Leida Chen
Publication:	Information & Management
Publisher:	Elsevier
Date:	January 2010
Copyright © 2010, Elsevier	

Logged in as:
Leslie Danjou

Order Completed

Thank you very much for your order.

This is a License Agreement between Leslie Danjou ("You") and Elsevier ("Elsevier"). The license consists of your order details, the terms and conditions provided by Elsevier, and the payment terms and conditions.

Get the printable license.

License Number	3434310769764
License date	Jul 22, 2014
Licensed content publisher	Elsevier
Licensed content publication	Information & Management
Licensed content title	Business–IT alignment maturity of companies in China
Licensed content author	Leida Chen
Licensed content date	January 2010
Licensed content volume number	47
Licensed content issue number	1
Number of pages	8
Type of Use	reuse in a thesis/dissertation
Portion	figures/tables/illustrations
Number of figures/tables/illustrations	All
Actual number of figures/tables/illustrations	11
Format	both print and electronic
Are you the author of this Elsevier article?	No
Will you be translating?	No
Title of your thesis/dissertation	Examining the Relationship Between IT Governance and Business Strategy Alignment
Expected completion date	Jan 2015
Estimated size (number of pages)	120
Elsevier VAT number	GB 494 6272 12

Permissions price	0.00 USD
VAT/Local Sales Tax	0.00 USD / 0.00 GBP
Total	0.00 USD

Complete Pages

Letter of Permission

Dr. Jerry Luftman
Global Institute for IT Management
Professor & Managing Director
1530 Palisade Ave, Suite 15L
Fort Lee, New Jersey 07024
Email: jluftman@globallim.com
Office: 201-787-9509 Skype: jerry.luftman
Web: http://www.globallim.com/

January 31, 2015

To Walden University:

The purpose of this letter is to grant Leslie D'Anjou permission to use my Strategic Alignment Maturity Model (SAMM) Instrument for the sole purposes of his Dissertation research at Walden University. If you have any questions and/or concerns, please feel free to contact me. Good Luck, Leslie!

Jerry Luftman Ph.D.
Professor & Managing Director
Global Institute for IT Management LLC

Include all Consent Forms:

_____

_____

_____

_____

Complete Pages

Appendix B: SAMM Survey Questions

Item	Question	Level1: With Process (No Alignment)	Level2: Beginning Process	Level3: Establishing Process	Level4: Improved Process	Level5: Optimal Process (Complete Alignment)
Communication maturity (COMM)						
COMM1	Degree of understanding of the business by the IT function	IT management lack understanding	Limited understanding by IT management	Good understanding by IT management	Understanding encouraged among IT staff	Understanding required of all IT staff
COMM2	Degree of understanding of IT by the business	Managers lack understanding	Limited understanding by IT management	Good understanding by managers	Understanding encouraged among staff	Understanding required of all staff
COMM3	Degree of richness of methods used for organizational learning	Casual communication and meetings	Newsletters, reports, group e-mail	Training, departmental meetings	Formal methods sponsored by senior management	Learning monitored for effectiveness
COMM4	Communication style used within the organization	Business to IT only; formal	One-way, somewhat informal	Two-way, formal	Two-way, somewhat informal	Two-way, informal and flexible
COMM5	Degree of knowledge sharing throughout the organization	Ad hoc	Some structured sharing emerging	Structured around key processes	Formal sharing at all levels	Formal sharing with partners
COMM6	Use of IT business liaisons	None or use only as needed	Primary IT-Business link	Facilitate knowledge transfer	Facilitate relationship building	Building relationship with partners
Competency and value maturity (COMP)						
COMP1	Focus of the metrics and processes to measure IT's contribution	Technical only	Technical cost, metrics rarely reviewed	Review, act on technical, ROI metrics	Also measure effectiveness	Also measure business cost, HR, partners
COMP2	Focus of the metrics and processes to measure business contribution	IT investments measured rarely, if ever	Cost/unit, rarely reviewed	Review, act on ROI, cost	Also measure customer value	Balanced scorecard, includes partners
COMP3	Degree of used orientation of integrated IT and business measures	Value of IT investments rarely measured	Business, IT metrics not linked	Business, IT metrics becoming linked	Formally linked, reviewed and acted upon	Balanced scorecard, includes partners
COMP4	Degree of service level agreements	Use sporadically	With units for technology performance	With units, becoming enterprisewide	Enterprisewide	Includes partners
COMP5	Frequency and formality of benchmarking practices	Seldom or never	Sometimes benchmark informally	May benchmark formally, seldom act	Routinely benchmark, usually act	Routinely benchmark, act on, and measure results
COMP6	Frequency and formality of IT assessments and reviews	Do not assess	Only when there is a problem	Becoming a routine occurrence	Routinely assess and act on findings	Routinely assess, act on, and measure results
COMP7	Degree of continuous improvement practices	None	Few, effectiveness not measured	Few, starting to measure effectiveness	Many, frequently measure effectiveness	Practices and measures well-established
COMP8	Contribution of IT to strategic goals	Ad hoc	Basic planning at the unit level	Some at organizational planning	Tasks when managed the enterprise	Integrated across and outside the enterprise
Governance maturity (GOV)						
GOV1	Degree of business strategic planning with IT involvement	Not done, or done as needed	At unit functional level, slight IT input	Some at cross-functional planning	At unit and enterprise, with IT	With IT, Partners
GOV2	Degree of IT strategic planning with business involvement	Not done, or done as needed	At unit functional level, slight business input	Some business input and cross-functional planning	At unit and enterprise, with business	With Partners
GOV3	Basis of budgeting IT resources	Centralized or decentralized	Cost/documented, some collection or Federal	Cost/documented or Federal	Federal	Federal
GOV4	Basis of IT investment decisions	CIO reports to CFO	CIO reports to CFO	CIO reports to COO	CIO reports to COO or CEO	CIO reports to CEO
GOV5	Frequency, formality, and effectiveness of IT steering committees	Cost center, spending is unpredictable	Cost center by unit	Some projects treated as investments	IT treated as investment	Profit center
GOV6	Integration of IT project prioritization	Reduce costs	Productivity, efficiency	Also a process enabler	Process driver, strategic enabler	Competitive advantage, profit
GOV7	IT function's responsiveness to changing business needs	Do not have	Most informally as needed	Formal, sometimes done regularly	Process to be effective	Also includes external partners

Complete Pages

Item	Question	Level1: With Process (No Alignment)	Level2: Beginning Process	Level3: Establishing Process	Level4: Improved Process	Level5: Optimal Process (Complete Alignment)
Partnership maturity (PART)						
PART1	Business' perception of the role of IT	React to business or IT need	Determined by IT function	Determined by business function	Mutually determined	Partners'/priorities are considered
PART2	Role of IT in strategic business planning	Cost of doing business	Becoming an asset	Enables future business activity	Drives future business activity	Partner with business in creating value
PART3	Integrated sharing of risks and rewards	Not involved	Enables business processes	Drives business processes	Enables or drives business strategy	IT, business adapt quickly to change
PART4	Formality and effectiveness of partnership programs	IT takes all the risks, receives no rewards	IT takes most risks with little reward	IT, business start sharing risks, rewards	Risks, rewards always shared	Managers incented to take risks
PART5	Perception of trust and value	IT-business relationship is not managed	Managed on an ad hoc basis	Processes exist but not always followed	Processes exist and complied with	Processes are continuously improved
PART6	Reporting level of business sponsor/champion	Conflict and mistrust	Transactional relationship	IT becoming a valued service provider	Long-term partnership	Partner, trusted vendor or IT provider
Technology scope maturity (SCOPE)						
SCOPE1	Technological and strategic sophistication of primary systems/applications	Usually none	Often have a senior IT sponsor or champion	IT and business sponsor or champion at unit level	Business sponsor or champion at corporate level	CIO is the business sponsor or champion
SCOPE2	IT standards articulation and compliance	Cost of doing business	Becoming an asset	Enables future business activity	Drives future business activity	Partner with business in creating value
SCOPE3	Degree of architectural integration	Not involved	Enables business processes	Drives business processes	Enables or drives business strategy	IT, business adapt quickly to change
SCOPE4	Degree of infrastructure transparency	IT takes all the risks, receives no rewards	IT takes most risks with little reward	IT, business start sharing risks, rewards	Risks, rewards always shared	Managers incented to take risks
SCOPE5	Degree of infrastructure flexibility	IT-business relationship is not managed	Managed on an ad hoc basis	Processes exist but not always followed	Processes exist and complied with	Processes are continuously improved
Skills maturity (SKILLS)						
SKILL1	Degree of an innovation culture	Discouraged	Somewhat encouraged at unit level	Strongly encouraged at unit level	Also at corporate level	Also with partners
SKILL2	Degree of integrated locus of power in IT-based decision	Top business and IT management in corporate	Same with emerging functional influence	Top business and unit management, IT advisor	Top business and IT management across firm	Top management across firm and partner
SKILL3	Degree of a change readiness culture	Tend to resist change	Change readiness programs	Programs in place at functional level	Programs in place at corporate level	Also proactive and anticipate
SKILL4	Degree of opportunity for skills enrichment through job transfer	Job transfers rarely occur	Occasionally occur within unit	Regularly occur for unit	Regularly occur at all unit levels	Also at corporate level
SKILL5	Degree of opportunity for skills enrichment through cross-training or job rotation	No opportunities	Decided by units	Formal programs run by all units	Also across enterprise	Also with partners
SKILL6	Degree of interpersonal interaction across IT and business	Minimal IT-business interaction	Strictly a business-only relationship	Trust and confidence is starting	Trust and confidence achieved	Attained with customer and partners
SKILL7	Ability to attract and retain IT staff with technical and business skills	No retention program, poor recruiting	IT hiring focused on technical skills	Technology and business focus, retention program	Formal program for hiring and retaining	Effective program for hiring and retaining

Questions

Comm1	To what extent does IT understand the organization's business environment (e.g., its customers, competitors, processes, partners/alliances)
Comm2	To what extent do the business organizations understand the IT environment (e.g., its current and potential capabilities, systems, services, processes)
Comm3	The following statements pertain to methods (e.g., intranets, bulletin boards, education, meetings, e-mail) in place to promote organizational education/learning (e.g., of experiences, problems, objectives, critical success factors). Organizational learning occurs primarily through
Comm4	The following question pertains to communications protocol. The IT and business communication style (e.g., ease of access,

Complete Pages

	familiarity of stakeholders) tends to be
Comm5	The following statements pertain to the extent in which there is knowledge sharing (intellectual understanding and appreciation of the problems/opportunities, tasks, roles, objectives, priorities, goals, direction, etc.) between IT and business
Comm6	The following statements pertain to the role and effectiveness of IT and business liaisons
Comp1	The following statements pertain to the metrics and processes used to measure IT's contribution to the business
Comp2	The following statements pertain to the use of business metrics to measure contribution to the business
Comp3	The following statements pertain to the use of integrated IT and business metrics to measure IT's contribution to the business
Comp4	The following statements pertain to the use of service level agreements (SLAs)
Comp5	The following statements pertain to benchmarking practices. Informal practices are such things as informal interviews, literature searches, company visits, etc., while formal practices are such things as environmental scanning, data gathering and analysis, determining best practices, etc.
Comp6	The following statements pertain to the extent of assessment and review of IT investments
Comp7	The following statements pertain to the extent to which IT-business continuous improvement practices (e.g., quality circles, quality reviews) and effectiveness measures are in place
Comp8	The demonstrated contribution that the IT function has made to the accomplishment of the organization's strategic goals is
Gov1	The following statements pertain to strategic business planning with IT participation
Gov2	The following statements pertain to strategic IT planning with business participation
Gov3	The following statements pertain to IT budgeting. Our IT function is budgeted as a
Gov4	The following statements pertain to IT investment decisions. Our IT investment decisions are primarily based on IT's ability to
Gov5	The following statements pertain to IT steering committee(s) with senior level IT and business management participation
Gov6	The following statements pertain to how IT projects are prioritized. Our IT project prioritization process is usually
Gov7	The ability of the IT function to react/respond quickly to the organization's changing business needs is
Part1	IT is perceived by the business as
Part2	The following statements pertain to the role of IT in strategic

	business planning
Part3	The following statements pertain to the sharing (by IT and business management) of the risks and rewards (e.g., bonuses) associated with IT-based initiatives (i.e., a project is late and over budget because of business requirement changes)
Part4	The following statements pertain to formally managing the IT/business relationship. To what extent are there formal processes in place that focus on enhancing the partnership relationships that exist between IT and business (e.g., cross-functional teams, training, risk/reward sharing)
Part5	The following statements pertain to IT and business relationship and trust
Part6	The following statements pertain to business sponsors/champions. Our IT-based initiatives
Scope1	The following statements pertain to the scope of your IT systems. Our primary systems are
Scope2	The following statements pertain to the articulation of and compliance with IT standards. Our IT standards are
Scope3	The following statements pertain to the scope of architectural integration. The components of our IT infrastructure are
Scope4	The following statements pertain to the level of disruption caused by business and IT changes (e.g., implementation of a new technology, business process, merger/acquisition). Most of the time, a business or IT change is
Scope5	The following statements pertain to the scope of IT infrastructure flexibility to business and technology changes. Our IT infrastructure is viewed as
Skills1	The following statements pertain to the extent the organization fosters an innovative entrepreneurial environment. Entrepreneurship is
Skills2	The following statements pertain to the cultural locus of power in making IT-based decisions. Our important IT decisions are made by
Skills3	The following statements pertain to your organization's readiness for change
Skills4	The following statements pertain to career crossover opportunities among IT and business personnel
Skills5	The following statements pertain to employee opportunities to learn about and support services outside the employee's functional unit (e.g., programmers trained in product/service production functions, customer service trained in systems analysis) using programs such as cross-training and job rotation. The organization

Complete Pages

Skills6	The following statements pertain to the interpersonal interaction (e.g., trust, confidence, cultural, social, and political environment) that exists across IT and business units in our organization
Skills7	The following statements pertain to the IT organization's ability to attract and retain the best business and technical professionals

There are five maturity levels for each question: Level 1 (no alignment with business processes), Level 2 (beginning process), Level 3 (establishing process), Level 4 (improved process), and Level 5 (optimal process – complete alignment).

Document your Survey:

Title of your Survey: _____

Survey Questions:

Appendix C: Letter of Recruitment

Leslie D'Anjou
Doctoral Candidate
School of Business
Walden University

Hello City Management Professionals,

My name is Leslie D'Anjou. I am an IT Business Analyst for the City of Goodyear and a Walden University Doctoral student. As part of my Walden University School's research project, I am requesting participation from Arizona cities, towns, and individuals to participate in a survey on IT/Business Alignment in local city government agencies.

This study will be relevant to you in several ways. Private sector organizations have been using this exact survey worldwide for over 14 years. Similarly, this survey is also applicable to local cities government agencies in terms of alignment between IT strategy and the agency's overall business strategy. As a participant, you will receive aggregate results from this study. These results will show how well a similar city of your size aligns and ways to improve alignment.

There are 41 online survey questions, which will take approximately 20 minutes to complete. We are asking participants to answer all questions based on their best judgment and perspective. Answering each survey question is valuable even if you may not know the actual answer. All participation is strictly voluntary. All personal or specific city information will remain confidential.

The target audience for this survey are City Management (CM Assistant, Deputy CM, CM, etc…), Department Heads (ITS, Finance, HR, Engineering, Economic Development, etc…), and Leaders (IT Subject Matter Experts, Supervisors, Managers, etc…). Participants will provide top management insight into what they perceive as the current alignment state of their city or town. This survey also targets a good cross section of cities and towns (small<400, medium 400<1,000, and large>1,000).

This study will show how well IT and business strategies are aligned based on five levels:

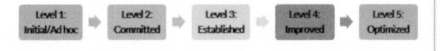

80

The goal of this survey is to provide you with information that may help in your organization improve misalignment. Misalignment can cause problems in IT/business strategic planning, budgeting, investment decisions, prioritization, and support.

This survey will be available at https://www.surveymonkey.com/r/ITBusAlignment. If you have any questions or concerns, please contact me.

Thank you in advance for completing the survey and your assistance with this study. Please feel free to share this survey with others as appropriate and encourage their participation.

Sincerely,

Leslie M. D'Anjou
Doctoral Candidate
School of Management
Walden University

81

Hello_____,

My name is Leslie D'Anjou, and I am a Ph.D. student in the School of Management at Walden University. I am contacting you again in hopes that you would participate in this study. I am conducting a study that examines the relationship between a city's IT/business strategic alignment and its employment size. This study focusses on the perception of business and IT professionals (BITPs), you.

There are 41 online survey questions, which will take approximately 20 minutes to complete. We are asking participants to answer all questions based on your best judgment and perspective. Answering each survey question is valuable even if you may not know the actual answer. All participation is strictly voluntary. All personal or specific city information will remain confidential.

If you are interested in participating in this study, this survey was available at https://www.surveymonkey.com/r/ITBusAlignment. If you have any questions and concerns, please contact me. Thank you much for your time and you participation. Have a great day.

Yours sincerely,

Leslie M. D'Anjou
Doctoral Candidate
School of Management
Walden University

Complete Pages

Appendix E: SurveyMonkey Acknowledgement Informed Consent Form

Welcome,

You are invited to take part in this research study based on the perception of top management in local city government agencies (LCGAs). Because you represent City Management (CM Assistant, Deputy CM, CM, etc...), Department Heads (ITS, Finance, HR, Engineering, Economic Development, etc...), or Leaders (IT Subject Matter Experts, Supervisors, Managers, etc...), your perspective is valuable in understanding business and IT alignment. This consent form allows you the opportunity to become informed of this study before taking this survey.

Leslie D'Anjou, a Business Analyst for the City of Goodyear led this Walden University research study.

Justification:
The problem researched in this study is the lack of information regarding IT/business strategic alignment level in LCGAs. The purpose of this study is to understand the perspective of top management business and IT professionals (BITPs) in local city government agencies (LCGAs). The goal is to identify the average alignment level of LCGAs by size (small <400, medium 400<1,000, large >1,000) to determine their next steps needed for improvement. This study has implications for positive social change in LCGAs by identifying maturity levels between IT and the overall business strategy.

Procedures:
· Read and accept the acknowledgment informed consent form before taking this online survey.
· Voluntarily participate in this online survey.
· Answer and complete all questions within this online survey and only complete one online survey per participant. This online survey will take approximately 20 minutes of your time.

Voluntary Nature of this Study:
All participation in this study is voluntary. Your decision to participate is entirely up to your discretion. No negative feedback was given if you decide not to take this online survey. Even if you have chosen to take this online survey and then decided that you did not want to complete it, you can stop. After submission, all completed surveys was used for this study.

83

Complete Pages

Benefits and Risks:

There is no rewards or compensation for taking this survey, but there are benefits for taking this online survey. It will:

1. Provide top management insight into how IT and the business aligns.
2. Offer knowledge about several maturity measures between IT and the business.
3. Increased knowledge of how to govern IT as it relates to the overall business strategy in LCGAs.
4. Provide the alignment level based on the size of the LCGAs.

There is no obligation, physical, or emotional risk in taking this online survey. Aggregate results were provided to all participating cities and towns. Participants can also obtain aggregate results upon email request.

Payment:

No payment was given for taking this survey.

Privacy:

All information gathered in this online survey will remain confidential. This study will not identify city names or personal information. It will only identify the size of your city's full-time employees and your job position. A memory stick that is password protected will store and secure electronic data for five years.

Contacts and Questions:

If you have any questions and concerns, please feel free to contact the researcher. If there is a need to speak privately about your rights as a participant, please contact Dr. Endicott, Director of the Institutional Review Board. She is the Walden University representative in which you can contact, Irb@waldenu.edu. Walden University's approval number for this study is 08-24-15-0133424, and it expires August 23, 2016.

Statement of Consent:

I have read the information above and feel that I understand this study well enough to make a voluntary decision. Based on the complete above mentioned information, I consent by clicking next below, of my accord, to participate in this research study. I am now ready and willing to take this online survey.

Complete Pages

Parts II through VII of this questionnaire assess your firm's current level of strategic alignment maturity by measuring your response to items related to your IT and business organizations:

Communications	(Part II)
Competency and value of IT	(Part III)
IT governance decisions	(Part IV)
Partnerships	(Part V)
IT infrastructure	(Part VI)
Skills resources	(Part VII)

For each of the questions in these sections, you are asked to choose the _one_ response that _most closely_ represents _your opinion_ of the _effectiveness_ of your organization's management practices and strategic choices. If you are unsure how to answer a question without guessing, or if the item is not applicable to your organization, mark the 'N/A or don't know' box.

You can now print or save this consent form. Please click Next below!

 2015.08.24 15:09:03 -05'00'

85

Abstract
Page

Take some time to submit this section to God!

Proverbs 3:6 (NIV) In all your ways submit to him, and he will make your paths straight.

Abstract Page

Writing an abstract should come at the end of your dissertation process. Knowing all the parts of writing your abstract is always a benefit. Your abstract should have these basic elements:

- Introduction (Opening) Sentence: Target an audience and state a desire. It should make a statement that inspires your reader to read more
- 2nd Sentence: Explain the effect of your stated desire
- 3rd Sentence: Write your problem statement. Your problem statement must be linked to your stated desire
- 4th Sentence: Write your purpose statement based on your survey participants
- 5th Sentence: Write about the theoretical framework of your study
- 6th Sentence: Write about your survey and analysis strategy
- 7th Sentence: Write about the instrument used and the results
- 8th Sentence: Explain the significance of your results
- 9th Sentence: Summarize your entire dissertation in one or two sentences

Write Your Abstract:

_____

_____

_____

_____

_____

_____

_____

_____

_____

_____

Complete Pages

Here is an example of my abstract:

Abstract

Top executives are interested in more transparent and formalized structures, applicable measurements, and clear justification of alignment. Limited or improper information technology governance (ITG) affects the business strategy that will ultimately influence the overall business alignment in local city government agencies (LCGAs). The problem addressed in this study was the lack of information regarding LCGAs IT/business strategic alignment maturity model (SAMM) level and the LCGAs' employment size. The purpose of this survey study was to evaluate 48 LCGA participants in the Southwestern part of the United States and compare their alignment perceptions with their cities' employment size. The theoretical framework for this study was based on ITG and business strategy as measured by the SAMM instrument. An online survey was used for data collection and data results were analyzed using descriptive statistics and an Analysis of Variance. After using the SAMM instrument, the current snapshot maturity level of LCGAs was 2.49 out of a maximum 5.0 level. Results illustrated no significant relationship between LCGAs alignment maturity levels and a city's size. This study empowers positive social change by providing LCGAs 6 incremental steps to improve the overall alignment maturity level in areas of transparent and formalized structures, applicable measurements, and improved alignment measures.

Complete Pages

Dedication Page

Take some time to submit this section to God!

Proverbs 3:6 (NIV) In all your ways submit to him, and he will make your paths straight.

Dedication Page

You can write your dedication page to anyone or thing that you would like.

Below is an example of my dedication page:

I dedicate this dissertation to Jesus Christ who deserves all the glory, honor, and praise for providing me this opportunity to reach this level of education. May I use all of God's blessings to fulfill my purpose here on earth!

Write Your Dedication:

_____

_____
_____
_____
_____
_____
_____
_____

90

Complete Pages

Acknowledgment Page

Take some time to submit this section to God!

Proverbs 3:6 (NIV) In all your ways submit to him, and he will make your paths straight.

Acknowledgment Page

I have used my acknowledgment page to say thanks. Is there persons in your life that you would like to thank? Write it in this section of your dissertation. You should consider thanking in paragraph form:

- Your immediate family
- Your Dissertation Committee
- Agencies
- Your University

Below is an example of my acknowledgment page:

Acknowledgments

My family has been my biggest supporter throughout this entire process. My wife, Angellicia D'Anjou, daughter, Avyannah D'Anjou, and son, Levi D'Anjou have been great supporters. Having my soul-mate, Angellicia, understand the time requirement demanded from a Ph.D. makes me more in love with her. She has been my balance throughout this entire process. She has given me just what I needed in love, support, understanding, patience, and leeway to dig-in and complete this journey. Thanks, much Honey! I love you with all my heart. Special thanks much also go out to my Dad and Mom, John & Ruth D'Anjou, who have been my voice of reason, prayer warriors, and support. I must also thank my two brothers and their families; John D'Anjou Jr., Santita D'Anjou, John D'Anjou III, and Johanna D'Anjou; along with James D'Anjou, Kessa D'Anjou, Ezra D'Anjou, and Eliana D'Anjou. Extended thanks must also go out to my Father-In-Law, Richard Schultz, Mother-In-Law, Joylin Harding, Brothers-In-Law, Philip Whyte, Sister-In-Law, Alisa Whyte, my little brother Aaron Schultz (expecting to call you Dr. Schultz soon), and my Aunty Judy Griffith.

Without the help of my Dissertation Chair and Committee members who contributed enormously, this would not have been plausible. My Team of two highly accomplished advisors has been my shoulders to lean on with answering questions, providing guidance, sharing insight and so much more. Many thanks go out to Dr. David Gould for being my Committee Chair, Faculty Advisor, and my guide to success. Many thanks also go out to Dr. Stuart Gold for verifying and validation my methodology.

Complete Pages

Finally, thanks to my URR, Dr. Nikunja Swain and my Forms and Styles reviewer, Dr. Travis Sands.

Many thanks must also go out to my team of supporters within LCGAs. Several city managers have gone far and beyond the call of duty. They have given me guidance, support, and mentorship that I'm much grateful and not worth to receive. Thank you both much! Much thanks go out to several others and everyone who have taken this survey and supported this study. Thank you all for your time and help.

Lastly, I would like to acknowledge Walden University for providing me with the vessel to attain this high honor in completing my Ph.D. The bold idea to have all Ph.D. Students focus on social change was and is tangible and attainable. All of the resources, user-friendly online classes, residencies, and knowledge gained have given me the ability to complete this great task. I would recommend Walden University to anyone who is looking for a high quality higher education. Through Walden, I was able to be in contact, work with, and gain invaluable insight from Dr. Luftman, the subject matter expert of the IT/business strategic alignment-maturity assessment tool. Thank you Dr. Luftman for taking your valuable time to spend it with me.

This entire process has been a great experience. Thank you all! Thank you, God!

Write Your Acknowledgment:

_____
_____
_____
_____
_____
_____
_____
_____
_____
_____

Complete Pages

Table of
Contents
Page

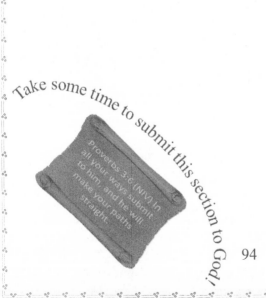

Take some time to submit this section to God!

Proverbs 3:6 (NIV) In all your ways submit to him, and he will make your paths straight.

Table of Contents Page

Use this page to insert your table of content based on your University's guidelines. Below is an example of my Table of Contents pages:

Table of Contents

Complete
Pages

97

Complete
Pages

Write Your Table of Content headings and subheadings:

_____
_____
_____
_____
_____
_____
_____
_____
_____
_____
_____
_____
_____
_____
_____
_____
_____
_____
_____
_____
_____
_____
_____

Complete Pages

List of Tables

Take some time to submit this section to God!

Proverbs 3:6 (NIV) In all your ways submit to him, and he will make your paths straight.

List of Tables

List all of your tables chronologically. As you insert a table into your dissertation, list them here into your list of tables. Below is an example of my list of tables:

Write Your List of Tables:

_____

_____

_____

_____

_____

_____

_____

_____

_____

_____

_____

_____

_____

_____

_____

_____

_____

Complete Pages

List of Figures

Take some time to submit this section to God!

Proverbs 3:6 (NIV) In all your ways submit to him, and he will make your paths straight.

List of Figures

List all of your figures within this section. Any figure or graphical display that you have entered into your dissertation, list it here within your list of figures. Below is an example of my list of figures:

List of Figures

Complete
Pages

Write your List of Figures:

_____

_____

_____

_____

_____

_____

_____

_____

_____

_____

_____

_____

_____

_____

_____

_____

_____

_____

_____

_____

_____

_____

_____

_____

_____

_____

_____

_____

Complete Pages

Title
Page

Take some time to submit this section to God!

Proverbs 3:6 (NIV) in all your ways submit to him, and he will make your paths straight.

Title Page

Your cover page must follow your University's guidelines. It should include your title, your name, your degrees, dissertation submission statement, the field of study, university, and year completed. Below is my title page example.

Assessing Information Technology and Business Alignment in Local

City Government Agencies

Leslie M. D'Anjou

MBA, DeVry University, 2008

BS, DeVry University, 2006

Dissertation Submitted in Partial Fulfillment

of the Requirements for the Degree of

Doctor of Philosophy

Management

Walden University

January 2016

Write Your Title Page:

Conclusion

Conclusion:

I remember completing my first draft of my proposal. It was exciting! The end was within reach. I was so proud of all the hard work that I have done. Approximately three weeks went by before I received feedback from my committee members. I opened their email and anxiously clicked on the attachment with their feedback. Shockingly, there were over 2,000 issues found. A hole could have opened and swallowed me. I was embarrassed, ashamed, and I felt worthless. I was hurt so much I did not know how to react. I sat there stunned.

After sitting at my computer for a while, several thoughts came to me. I thought, "this could take months to fix and complete. Goddddddddddd! I need to take a break from all of this. Is this worth it?" As I was trying to think about what was next, another thought came to me. You can fix these errors tonight!" I got excited. Could it be possible? I took on the challenge and was able to fix all those errors that very night. I only had two total revisions for my proposal.

There are many obstacles that you will face while doing your dissertation. Having a good starting point, completing each chapter, and completing your pages are three simple steps to get it done successfully. Don't you dare give up. I believe that what separates a person who completes their doctorate and those who do not is perseverance. If you give up, you will never complete it. Get it done!

Proverbs 3:6 (NIV) In all your ways submit to him, and he will make your paths straight.

When you feel like you can't do this anymore, turn to God for help. He promises to make your path straight, but there is process involved. God said that He will. It is a process. I believe that you can do it. I know that if you persevere, God will be right there with you and He will make your path straight. Get it done!

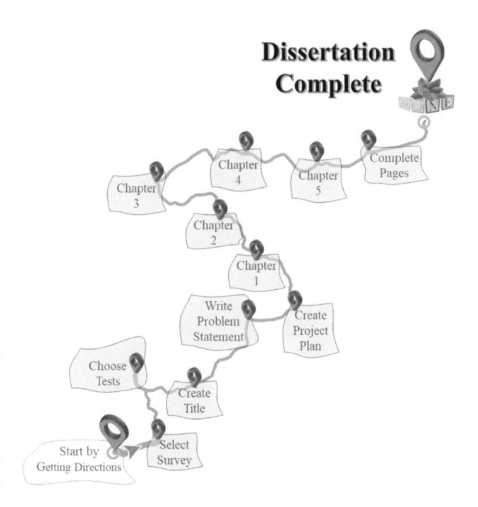

Dissertation
Complete

Chapter 4
Chapter 5
Complete Pages
Chapter 3
Chapter 2
Chapter 1
Write Problem Statement
Create Project Plan
Choose Tests
Create Title
Start by Getting Directions
Select Survey

Notes:

Notes:

Acknowledgments

Thanks be to God for allowing me this opportunity to write. God, He is so wonderful. I owe everything to Him. I will serve You all my days. Thank you much…

- Thanks to my Wife, Angellicia D'Anjou for being my backbone throughout it all. You are the best Wife and soulmate ever. You inspire me to greatness. I love you always!
- Thanks to my kids, Avyannah Malia D'Anjou and Levi Joshua Leslie D'Anjou. You motivate me to do good. Always hear God's voice and do all that He wants you to do.
- Thanks to my parents, John D'Anjou Sr. and Ruth D'Anjou. You have always been my Godly examples in which I can model myself after. Thanks to my Mother-In-Law, Joylin Harding for being a great support. I love you all always.
- Thanks to my brothers John D'Anjou Jr. and James D'Anjou for always being close friends. Much respect!
- Thanks to Santita D'Anjou, Kessa D'Anjou, Alisa Schultz, and Aaron Schultz for being great stepsisters and stepbrother.
- Thanks to nephews and nieces John D'Anjou III, Esra D'Anjou, Johanna D'Anjou, and Eliana D'Anjou for keeping me young.
- Thanks to my Church, Skyway, for allowing me the opportunity to co-pastor our youth with my Wife. Much thanks to all the Pastors, leaders, and youth for your prayers and support.
- Thank you, Apostles Drs. Greg and Dawn Brown. Your discipleship and friendship have been invaluable.
- Thank you Grand Cannon University (GCU) for your support and inspiration to teach from a Christian Worldview, love it.
- Thank you to all my extended family, friends, and Military buddies for all your support.

Thank you all!!!

About Author

Dr. Leslie D'Anjou is a devoted Christian. He loves the Lord with all of his heart, soul, and mind. He is committed to doing the things of God.

He loves spending time with his family, pastoring youth, teaching at the university, and having fun. He is married to his soulmate Angellicia, have a daughter Avyannah that is 8 years old, and a son Levi that is 5 years old. On Sundays and Wednesdays, he gladly serves the Youth at his local church, Skyway. He loves teaching Business Statistics & IT at Grand Cannon University. Every Saturday, if he has the time, you can find him playing Tennis all morning long.

He holds a Ph.D. in Management with an emphasis on Information Systems Management (ISM) from Walden University. He also holds an MBA specializing in Project Management and Information Systems Management from Keller Graduate School of Management. He has a bachelor's degree from DeVry University in Technical Management majoring on Networking.

Dr. D'Anjou owes his life to God and is devoted to sharing his life's testimony with everyone that will listen.

Index